Lost Songs &
Last Chances

Lost Songs &
Last Chances

Poems

CHRIS RANSICK

A Division of Samizdat Publishing Group

CONUNDRUM PRESS A Division of Samizdat Publishing Group.
PO Box 1353, Golden, Colorado 80402

Lost Songs & Last Chances

Conundrum Press Edition

Copyright © 2015 by Chris Ransick.

For information, email INFO@CONUNDRUM-PRESS.COM.

ISBN: 978-1-942280-20-0
Library of Congress Control Number: 2014959790

Conundrum Press books may be purchased with bulk discounts for educational, business, or sales promotional use. For information please email: info@conundrum-press.com

Conundrum Press online: CONUNDRUM-PRESS.COM

ACKNOWLEDGMENTS

Thanks go out to the editors of the following journals who first published these poems, in existing or previous versions:

Pilgrimage, "Bread & Anger: A Poem"; *Fugue*, "How I Swam to the Bottom of the Ocean"; *Copper Nickel*, "Curfew"; *The Denver Post*, "On the Bank of the Nameless River"; *Denver Syntax*, "Poem for Your Shoes" and "The Angry Man Eats Lunch Alone"; *Appalachia*, "Evening Rain, Red Sand"; *The Eleventh Muse*, "Summertail" and "Rondeau for Late Winter"; *Paterson Literary Review*, "Elvis Comes Back"; *The Red Wheelbarrow*, "At the Discount Store in Durango, Colorado"; *Marginalia*, "The Defenseman's Lament" and "Poison Words"; *Staten Island Review*, "Black Calendar" and "Sonata"; *Treasure House*, "Snowfall, Suburbia"; *Calliope*, "Harbinger, Past Midnight"; *Evergreen Living*, "A Place Called Independence"; *Coyote Kiva*, "Elegy for Rosa"; *Vol.No.*, "Toxicosis"; *Crab Creek Review*, "Backroad Roadkill"; Colorado Center for the Book and Now It's Up to You Press, "Tom Ferril's Mandolin"; and *Convolvulus*, "Standing in the Street."

Thanks to the editors and judges of *Fugue* for awarding "How I Swam to the Bottom of the Ocean" 2nd prize in their annual poetry contest; and to the editors and judges of the *Paterson Literary Review* at the Poetry Center in Passaic, N.J. for granting "Elvis Comes Back" an honorable mention in the Ginsberg Poetry Awards.

for Sean & Kelsey
my best songs

TABLE OF CONTENTS

I was lost
And sang my broken-down songs in the hell of the hour.
Then in my heart moved an oar,
And I was found by a breeze from a door in the sea of forms
And was rowed to the cherry trees on the shore.

Selah. Selah.

—Stan Rice

Bread & Anger: A Prayer

Arguments at home happen most often in the kitchen.
—Anonymous

Maybe the bananas, forgotten and going
blotchy brown, give off a subtle fume,
causing your spouse to hurl the

wooden spoon, turn on her heel and scream
obscenities, a tirade so profound, needles
twitch across seismic scrolls in nearby

laboratories and squirrels in the elms
scurry for their nests. Maybe salmon,
sealed in plastic, nestled in darkness,

spasm again in a flood of light as you
open the freezer door, flicking tails
as if to leap up roaring, frigid falls,

remembering how it was to swim
under falling snow and moonlight
into a net spread out like revenge.

Teenagers' milk-washed cereal bowls,
discarded in a rush for school,
may harbor sugary curses, the residue

of a thousand times "No." Old salt
may lose its flavor, each crystal imbued
with the taste of a wish unvoiced.

To sprinkle it on soup releases
essence of snow from a failed ski trip
or taste of paint chips off shabby walls.

That blob of carbon on the oven floor—
a cherry pie that oozed one August night—
now absorbs abandoned dreams.

The table tilts under the weight of
telephone, garbage, utility bills,
credit card offers, bright catalogs.

where models march, impossibly slender
midriffs bare, skin smooth as an
airbrushed memory of youth.

O kitchen, troubled soul of the house,
let the aroma of fresh-baked bread
overcome all bitter scents and leave us

this once at peace, hands touching hands
as we pass the plates, in communion
one more night with those we love.

Tom Ferril's Mandolin

From these rooms, your notes would fall
through summer nights, into back yards
where old men leaned against a wall

to talk, to sit in cool dusk playing cards.
Sandburg strummed a guitar, going round
a tune through which you weaved, the words

and strings together shaping sound.
I would have smiled to hear those songs
from a nearby porch, verses crooned

by two poets in their cups. Today I found a ring
of flagstone under dirt while we cleared
decades of weeds out back, wrongs

grown tall by time and neglect. The rock shone red
when rinsed with water and sun. Someone told how
Dorothy Parker woke up in your daughter's bed,

hung over and in need of a poem. Now,
the rooms have no beds. Heat swirls in the loft
above the rounded desk at the window

where you made books, an ancient craft.
This house will never fall silent
though the music grows ever more soft.

Suite for Lost Friends

1. Heading for the Coast

I will help lift the piano
into the van, to rest beside
the couch when you leave tomorrow
with the wind, which passes for tide
on the plains. The mountains will loom
in your mirrors, recede as you roam

west. The seagulls know you're coming.
Monterey cypress lean away from salt
spray above rocks where waves' drumming
sounds the edge at which all roads halt.
When you arrive, stand at the sea
and speak of our friendship, tell how we

passed the long hours of winter
heating kettles of brew, old songs
a compliment to our banter.
We're older now; we know all wrongs
cannot be righted, nor all wounds
healed. I've a new one. It resounds.

2. Running Again

This morning's grief
burns behind my eyes,
a wound I'll always have,
opening in the skin,
exposing ankle bone.
Friend, I felt the warmth
leave your body, prone
but no longer in pain.
It spread through my palms
and then we were running again
through a ravine, pine-drenched
winter wind a perfume
mingled with hoarfrost
on your wolf-coat.
In the end, this is the story of
how I became more like you
and understood the animal
in man, the gentle part.

3. The Space Between Here and Morning

my friend falls asleep   on the floor
          of my room, curled
around a dream of black   hair   cascading

out of blacker night   terrible
          when hands tremble, when tongues
can't find familiar words

scattered   far back
          in the throat
mornings when fog   spills

off low hills, hands trembling because   to touch
          a woman's smooth skin, even
out of love   or in   is different

than to imagine touching   he falls
          asleep, fitful and broken
a glass so thin he fills but   halfway   shatters

and I gather him, my arms   strong
          enough, my words
not hard to find, though   bolting,

nervous birds when I approach,   hands
          extending over
the figure of my friend   as if cupping

medicine, soothing water   pure
          and carried far
from a place where no one   ever dreams

4. *When They Found Her Sister*

On the last day of winter, even as
grass shoots pushed through old sod and
the elm's swollen buds released gold dust
when squirrels leaped branch to branch,
on that day they found her, eyes closed
in sleep, not breathing: cold, gone.
For those who wish to die in bed
among dreams, when one can penetrate
the mist and enter death slowly, at peace
with all things, this is the image
of gentle goodbye. Her hands clasped
the sheet as if it were just night's chill
that filled the room, not the heat leaving
her soft shoulder forever. Spring
will send no mourners. The crocus
and phlox will bloom pale purple
as though their roots weren't sunk in loam
made from the bodies of things. Children
will still run squealing in the park,
chasing their days down the slope toward
a future they cannot know. She was
such a child once, her skin as supple,
her laughter the timbre of chimes,
her bones strong enough to last.

5. The Last Laugh
for P.J.

I saw you walking the stairs, your bad leg
slowing you down, and heard your sore lungs

clutch with coughing. What did I miss?
Was there another clue, maybe your eyes

going darker brown as summer ended?
Now that light is gone and nothing

opens the door to your room,
not even the right key. I see sunlight

bang on your window all afternoon
but I don't believe it wants in.

There's weeping in the halls and I'm
going out now, down past it all, home,

but the day is destroyed with you.
I won't be able to forget how we sat together

just days ago, talking of a January
you won't see. The snow will come,

I'm sure of that. I'll try to remember
laughing with you, the way it was.

6. *Poison Words*

Out of the burls of dying trees, cruel words seep,
spreading across the frost-burned grass at night,
flowing uphill, against reason, against a brother.

There is no obstacle curses cannot leap,
no door they cannot burst open with the weight
of everything past. It's ancient jealousy, no other

reason, that pulls black language from deep
wounds. Sun would banish hate with its light
but these words, spoken only in dark, wither

the last green leaves from ash and maple, reap
rotten fruit from forgotten plants, blight
those few late blooms that will bloom no further.

In your own heart, this memory keep:
a broad field, two men stand at the edge of sight,
this poem the only tether.

7. *Upon Hearing That a Friend is Ill*
for Ted

When we write of these things, you and I,
there is never any reason, only the sound—
bells ringing out across a port, the sky,
the things we write of, you and I.
The hot blue of noon burns, but try
to find the end of the circle; once found,
we will write of these things, you and I.
There is never any reason, only the sound.

8. John the Pressman

Truth is, if you love your job
he told me one March afternoon,
then work's a joy. Thirty years

he ran the sheet-feed Heidelberg,
its arm swooping, snatching,
pulling paper under the lowering plate,

another sheet, another sheet.
There was the time that Ernie Walsh
forgot and leaned into the swing arm—

knocked him flat on his ass. We thought
he'd died at first, the blood and all,
but he came back a wiser man.

I watched the old man's face
while he laughed his distant laugh,
the spring breeze catching us both

in a momentary chill just as he
confessed how badly he
missed his friends,

the times they'd had. *But even more,*
I miss the press, he said, a sad smile
etching lines deep into his face.

I'd run that thing all day and know
I'd done a good day's work. John
the pressman shook his head

and leaned into the wind.
Just remember, you miss most
those things that you did best.

9. *Sonata*

for Chuck

this field empty of
everything

but weeds sprouting
downward, buds

in frozen sod
stalks

of long grass brittle
to wish

for that music again
drifting

from your upstairs window
moonlight

sonata, the first
movement

and last motion of
your hands

rolling, punctuating
just

about to cease
to wish

winter would descend
once

on a summer night
and summer

bulge up through this
ice

just once
yes

Sleeping in the Dead Boy's Room

The bed's been made for these two years,
quilted comforter blue and gray
covers a well of sadness. His mother's tears

filled up the well. The last thin light of day
gilds a trophy on the dresser top—
the baseball player lets fall his bat to pray

for the souls of all boys who try, but drop
fly balls in lonely fields. Certificates
mark years until achievements stop

suddenly, and then—no more dates.
In a color photograph he grins,
a lanky boy, arms slung around his mates

standing by the car's sprung door, groans
of laughter over some bad joke
erased from the scene by invisible winds.

Near the closet, his bathrobe hangs on a hook.
The pillow has a curious dent and springs sag
and creak as if the bed, long mute, now speaks

its shrill regrets. The dog's tail won't wag
for strangers, though he watches the door,
unclear about the residents, suitcase and bag

unpacked, unfamiliar shoes on the floor.
Outside, winter night pulls the last heat
off the desert and flees, still wanting more.

Custodian's Night Song

Alone each night, I come to walk these halls
with mop in hand, with giant garbage can.
I sing for all the faces on the walls,
my chorus is the ventilation fan.

With mop in hand, with giant garbage can,
I clean the rooms of educated men.
My chorus is the ventilation fan,
my song transports me where I've never been.

I clean the rooms of educated men,
I wipe away the residue of days.
My song transports me where I've never been,
to beaches where I bask in summer rays.

I wipe away the residue of days,
I swab the urinals until they shine
like sun on beaches washed in summer rays.
I don't mind work; to labor so is fine.

I swab the urinals until they shine
and clear the trash from underneath the sink.
I don't mind work; to labor so is fine.
The quiet gives me so much time to think.

I sing for all the faces on the walls
while all alone each night I walk these halls.

Suite for an American Boyhood

1. Asleep on Seward's Couch

I remember light so dim
each mirror in the tiny room pulled
my eyes toward shadows and voices,
vague shapes trapped since
Lincoln was shot and Seward
viciously stabbed, the assassin's blade
nicking and sparking on the
metal brace encircling his neck.

Our teacher said the Secretary was
therefore saved by the accident
weeks before the attack when a
spooked horse tossed him from his carriage.
Days and nights he lay on a couch,
waiting to heal, in pain, tended
by family. We saw a replica carriage
parked forever in a shed as though

awaiting another horse and slow procession.
In Washington, Booth had wedged one door
shut, crept across the hall and sprung
another to the balcony, surprise
and distraction his friends, a slug
of lead for Abe. He leapt in his spurs,
catching the flag, falling, shattering his shin.
Above the stage, blood poured

over chair's fabric, that doomed man's war,
bitter as all wars, finally over.
But Seward survived. His assassin's neck
refused to snap some months later

when the floor of the scaffold fell away,
so he slowly strangled, as if
dying meant something. Our teacher's
monologue reached for the past but I

felt live things in the room among those
boys and girls silent with the sense
only children have of the dead in their houses,
lying still in beds but not asleep
as we know it, not the ghosts of books
and bad films, more like the marble tops
of tombs in great cathedrals. The teacher
turned and led them out, every kid

except me. I had to lie on that couch, slip
into the stone skin of Seward, his severe face
staring out of portraits everywhere.
The shelves of books lent symmetry
to the walls, the window admitted
gray-green light as the sounds of the group
receded down the hall, taking with them
time and all the noise of a century.

2. Prayer for a Mantis

Concealed in curls of shade
under leaves or clinging to a twig,

you could have been as fierce
as any alien if we'd been cicadas

or katydids instead of boys
with Mason jars. Your green wings

folded into fans on your back,
pulsing, pulsing,

and that terrible wedge of head
set with onyx eyes—

the last vision of grasshoppers
held in the vise of your claws.

Devil's Riding Horse, soothsayer,
we hadn't guessed your legendary greed.

We watched as your antennae
twirled like stiffened whips,

sensing each doomed cricket
gathered from a nearby field and

dropped into your jar. We were
little Romans at a glass Coliseum,

and when your prey began to spring,
wild to escape the close confines,

your arms would unclasp from prayer
and strike, grasp the victim

like an ear of corn
you chewed down to the cob,

still live and kicking.
You never left a crumb.

Gluttony finally got you.
We didn't know to stop

serving that feast. You ate
until your sleek gut swelled

and ceased its slow pulsing
and you leaned into glass, arms

twitching at phantom flyers
until your final flinch.

Then my friends scattered home
to dinner and mothers more tame

than any lady mantis ever was.
I shook your fragile frame

into my palm, filling it.
Destroyer, did I kill you?

Since then I've tried to learn your prayer
for patience, what I would need

if bread were winged and I were starved,
my hands like nets or weapons.

Some nights I sit again in the grass
near the rotting fence slats,

hoping to coax one of your kind
out of secrecy, into my garden,

to stalk beneath the vegetable canopy
and clean up the neighborhood.

3. Sitting in Grandmother's Kitchen

It's a June morning in Cincinnati. I'm
sitting in a pool of enamel and
linoleum, my grandmother's kitchen.

But the mother of my father is long dead
and this kitchen lives only in my mind, a memory
saved like the last page of a good book

to read again this day, to remember
the pleasure and the slanting sun
falling through the faded curtains

down to the tabletop, so bright my eyes
squint involuntarily. My grandmother
pours hot water over teabags, one

in each of the cups set out
on the table before us, yellow cups
doubly bright in yellow sun, and she

croons a rhyme in that Irish voice, every
consonant soft as if her lips and tongue
were made of melting butter,

and I realize now, though I didn't then,
she loved little boys because
children were the only gifts she received.

I want to ask her about the stories
behind her eyes, I want to ask for another song,
but I didn't then and cannot now.

I want to touch her hand, skin softer
than the surface of a brook, but I can't
get back to that kitchen in the sun

except in the memory, a rippling time
that allows no touches nor words
that never did occur. Someday I'll be

a grandfather, big hands, belly
like a barrel, voice deep and gruff,
rhymes lapping at a child's ears the way

a great bear licks its muddy cub
and then I can make the moment
a memory forever of hands touching

and songs sung twice, stories told over
and over so the words, like gold,
never tarnish down long years.

4. *The Crying Trees*

I see the crumpled body of
a bird beneath the crying trees.

Two wounds that rub,
two foreign limbs
have thrown their fruit down on the ground.

The cherry pit, the apple core,
rotting in a hollow sit.

My mother's lips behind the glass
move mute as her hand dips into

soapy water, yarn unwinding,
leaving just her ring, a silver
shine beneath the crying trees.

Two wounds that rub,
two tongues entwined,
the wind is nudging at their sides.

I carry stones, my pockets bulge,
I argue back and forth with bones

of a rabbit chewed apart by dogs,
entrails scattered on the snow.

Thick sinews red, still warm to touch,
I stir them gently with a stick.

The pawprints, red, grow fainter as
across the ice and mud they go

until they stop. I look among
the branches tangled at the top,

two wounds that rub,
the wooden flesh
that never recognizes me.

I wake to hear the crying trees,
I lie among the roots and fear

the upward thrust of trunk, the musk
of leaves that blacken at the base,

but just one voice
but just one voice
and two wounds rubbing faces.

5. The House of Gilbert Treat

This is the house of Gilbert Treat.
When you enter it moves beneath your feet,

the banister curving away like a fish,
its dark oak railing worn by hands.

Look down the hall that seems to stretch
away and down, away and down.

The house of Gilbert Treat has rooms
that never have seen the light of day:

a reading room, poorly lit,
a skin of dust atop the books.

Out on the porch it's cold to wait,
between the hip-high drifts of snow,

ignoring the ivy, out of control,
writhing across brown chimney bricks,

bushes rising like burial mounds a
pattern amid an unpatterned yard.

The house of Gilbert Treat, you know
opens like others at the door,

at the end of the day,
at the end of the year,

at the end of the block where cornfield stubs
thrust up through the glossy crust.

They beckon to you, knowing your fear
as you stand before the enormous door,

and hear his footsteps
coming slow.

6. Ghost Runners

August morning, languid sun
not yet fierce, cool air hovering
over slick outfield green

and infield dirt pocked
by a thunderstorm,
flashing from the far side

of last night's dreams.
Two boys arrive, tousled hair, cutoffs,
bats nailed and taped together,

carried over narrow shoulders.
One tosses a ball with his
free hand, sends it sailing toward

pitcher's mound, where it rolls
to a stop against chewed rubber.
They laugh, take seats on the

dilapidated bleachers while
overhead a great crow
lifts off from the copse of elms

and circles, harassed by blackbirds.
Summer is waning
but not gone. Sumac,

pendulous in shade, await
ripening sun. Three more boys
emerge from a wooded path, chatter

a song fading too soon.
Another arrives in a flash, abandons
his still-rolling bike.

Six is enough if you
close right field and use ghost runners,
make pitcher's mound good as first.

Boys grapple a bat; the winner yells
We get Frankie, you get Matt.
The smallest kid pounds his glove as

squads form and one takes the field—
pitcher, shortstop, deep left center.
The ball is near new, white leather

marked with a dark scuff
from the swing that sent it foul,
deep in the weeds yesterday.

This time the batter connects clean—
tock! echoing down years.
In slow motion, all six boys

animate, runner toward first,
teammates leaping, pitcher turning
to watch the ball fly, shortstop

in the grass for a cutoff throw.
In left, the fielder turns and runs,
eyes skyward, for the farthest place.

High Mountain Disc Golf

Four new discs: silver, orange, blue and cream.
Two teens, both grown out of their skins,
lope like cougars over prickly pear and
leap from dust-dulled rock.

Their mother stands beside you on a
concrete tee, laughing softly
as though everything were funny:
daredevil swallows, dragonflies, heat rising

in whorls up the slope. The kids
have thrown, daughter into a scrub pine,
son into oblivion, a wicked long drive
over the ravine where a cool stream winds.

You throw yours in, hoping
to bathe your feet. Low summer sun
marks a long day but there's time yet
to finish the course.

Ten thousand steps will take you
to evening, but also to another place.
How will you ever say goodbye well enough?
Now's not the time, and you walk

down the ravine's soft edge, the water
beckoning, the silver disc you threw
glistening in a pool. It's a clear shot
to the hole. The three of them watch from above.

I'd Like to Come

I'd like to come to the
gathering in your field,

see the women dance, hair
swirling out like riverwater.

Some crows in that
particular cottonwood know

my name and will hold me
to a promise I once made.

I'd like to come and sleep
under swaths of stars, croon

to the breeze about its next
assignment, spread music

across the sandstone, chant
words without meaning to

interfere. I'd like to come
and maybe, if the sun forgives

my labors here, if the crickets
will scratch long enough to

hide my escape, then I'll appear
at the edge of your vision,

wriggling like a shaman from
among the willows.

Mountains & Plains Suite

1. A Place Called Independence

The portal's wood, weathered by
a hundred winters, sags, extrudes
tortured, rusty nails

never to be buried again
out of incessant wind surging
as autumn afternoon fails.

The rutted road, a wagon's path
unhealed all these years,
divides delicate tundra.

Roofs of tilting hovels have collapsed
to plank floors and last light
glints off glass shards, dull shades

of green and gray, miner middens
made of bottles whose brew soothed
visions of cave-ins, hard rock, lodes

gone dry. Spring's roaring water
must have sluiced men's despair
down those rock gullies,

boulders breaking loose, tumbling,
punctuating the scattered taunts
from a thousand chips of scree.

The mill wheel, kinetic, stilled,
will never turn again. No voices
will rise after night falls

except those that whisper of loss
with numb lips, waiting for brief summer
to thaw from your shoulder the shroud.

2. Evening Rain, Red Sand

Even as the sun fails, it lights
at last the sandstone arch,

falls on the faint blue canyon sage,
and drips from the branches

of the pygmy forest.
It also falls

upon my brother
resting his swollen joints

on red Navajo sand.
The first drops spatter

dark patches near his cheek,
and he slips into the tent to sleep.

3. Hummingbird Ballet

Linden, piñon, cholla, sage,
scent of horses and rain on dirt
perfume wind's soft surge

across your skin. Two birds flirt
at the feeder's edge, one chasing away
his rival with rapid chirrups,

then returning to hover and dart, red clay
across the valley the same hue
as his throat. Another joins the fray

and they flit off into blue.
Just one returns, wings abuzz, beak
dipping down for sugary brew.

4. *Wapiti in the Meadow*

Pale rumps upturned to sun
move across the meadow.

Mouths to grass, elk lick the slope's
mud for minerals—

copper, salt, potassium, iron.
The dirt releases incense,

spring runoff raising marshes,
braiding toward the river.

Brittle grass crackles under
cloven hooves, impressions

slowly filling. Three mule deer
join the herd, slender and small,

ears more delicate, flickering
at every shift in wind.

Scat lies everywhere on the trail
alongside water that bubbles, electric.

Bones of old wapiti hide
among willows where one

lurches to its knees, slides a flank
low and folds limbs to rest,

although always ready to spring
and flash for the cedar grove.

Its head swivels, side-set eyes
scanning the rim of the canyon.

5. On the Bank of the Nameless River

In the end, all rivers are nameless,
just as currents folding back and back
where water bends against the bank
are nameless, the water itself different
and indifferent in that crook
of river, though ripples repeat shape,
change ceaselessly. Chunks of sandstone
lie nameless. Cottonwoods rising on sand spits
splitting the water may have names
but ones I'll never know. A red fox
hunting the riverbottom this May morning
does not call her prey by name nor
name her pups, nourished on blood
milled in anonymous bones.
Spring's first crickets scratch
from tall grass on the bank a descant
to the river's full-throated song
as wind throbs through willows
and sweeps down-valley, carrying tales
off the fractured black peak, and all of it
is nameless. What would I call this place?
What voice could join these harmonies
and last as long as water and wind?
From now on, I will go nameless,
without fear of vanishing,
listening for my feet upon earth.

6. Mill Creek, August Morning

Rain wakes sage, then cool wind
pulls scent from silver stems

to paint morning. Pronghorn pause,
tensed along the fenceline.

Such silence. You can hear the wind
approach, arrive, move off

down the canyon's contour, dispersing
to gather again beyond the rim.

On high slopes, chaparral survives.
Great pines with room to sway slough

mottled cream and orange bark,
sap-heavy, a welcoming duff

to lie upon and breathe in summer
slipping toward autumn's pass.

7. Morning Comes to Outlaw Cave

Dawn draws indigo from night sky,
and color paints the canyon walls
while overhead the raptors fly,

keen eyes search as they cruise by,
they leave behind their piercing calls.
Dawn draws indigo from night sky

and first light strikes the canyon, dry
where cool rain so rarely falls.
Still, overhead the raptors fly.

Coiled snakes under willows lie
where they will wait till daylight stalls.
Dawn draws indigo from night sky.

Thin clouds disperse, the sun mounts high
as rainbows weave through river pools
and overhead the raptors fly,

the earthbound fearing claw and eye.
Green water sings on waterfalls,
dawn draws indigo from night sky,
while overhead the raptors fly.

8. A Close-Banked Fire

Dusk brings a late spring chill
down from high slopes where it hid
during afternoon sun's reign.
We've gathered wood,
wrist-thick limbs and
matchstick tinder, a tuft or two
of dry moss and pine needles.
His patient hands compose a frame.
No rush. The flame will grow,
coaxed higher by darkness stripping
green and blue from earth and sky.
I snap sticks and load clumsily,
almost smothering flames. Wordlessly
he lifts the nest, lets in oxygen and
the wood rekindles, blazes bright.
Heat builds and radiates; I strum
an old guitar and he breathes
a harmonica to life so softly,
fish cease swimming, float

with Shoshone's current. The fire
burns low but bright enough
to warm my fingers on the strings.

9. Ten Scenes from the Legacy of Buffalo Bill

Ladies and gentlemen, look left and you'll see all that remains of
        Bill Cody's turkey ranch—his first big venture.

See that rusted-out car, circa 1930? That marks the edge of the
        ancient buffalo jump that's now the county dump.

Cody fought the Cheyenne and took the scalp from their
        young chief, Yellow Hand!

His circus performed mock battles in Marseilles and Rome.

Don't forget to visit the museum to see his Colt revolver and
        a replica of the medal Congress revoked.

Nobody could match Bill Cody. He killed four thousand buffalo
        in one month alone!

There's the trace of the old Indian trail to Red Lodge, right
        there where the banks come low at water's edge.

Look, young ravens in a nest high on the cutbank cliffs!

Don't forget your souvenir photographs, taken on
        Little Drop Rapids, just ten dollars.

Oh, never mind that. It's the EPA monitoring an
        abandoned oil refinery.

10. Blue Heron, Riverbend

I saw you at the river's edge,
perched on a dun rock sunken
among willows, blue-gray feathers
carved in dusty stone. Frantic geese
thrashed, wingtips slapping water
as they rose; you never flinched.
Your long neck held its arch,
eyes keen for a flashing fish.

An hour I watched
from a shrinking patch
of rare November sun
until shade chilled my back
and sent me home along the path.

11. Loneliness on Sandia Mountain

Count the sage bushes on the mesa. No hawks
ever swooped above without scattering remorse.

I toss the husk of a dream upon the sand
and wait for wind to chase it away.

January air burns skin, a cold
sleeping snakes will never know.

I would be Coyote on this mesa, trick
crow out of his feathers, press the milk

from the cactus for my thirst as
low sun rolls shadows behind piñon,

lights far peaks, bright snow inviting
the eyes of dead men and the lonely.

Who could ever sing as sadly as the
dry creek? Does blue sky blaze cruel

in winter so sandstone can hold
the noon heat until dark?

I remove my heart, hold it, lay it down
in a hollow of that smooth stone.

12. *February Twilight, Lost Miner Ranch*

Catlike, a creature moves
across the field, belly-deep
in drifts. Three horses

at the far fence don't bolt,
but surely their eyes,
like mine, are turned to this.

Soon, a weak sun will fall finally
silent and a gibbous moon will
blow pale blue from the sky

across the snow. Soon,
late winter will forgive the creek
for trickling toward spring

and relinquish all its ice.
But this night, all holds fast,
thaw-songs captured in turf.

13. *Driving Kenosha Pass, April Morning*

Wet, heavy snow clings to every surface,
vertical and horizontal.
Pines slough clots of white, releasing
wisps into unseen wind, and low sun
casts long shadows across the road.
Spumes of ice crystals swirl over vacant fields,
cattle trails knotting in muddy wallows and
along fence lines. Swallows and crows
swing out of the sky, a darting flash of wings
around slow paddling black boats, circling,
waiting till cars pass to descend to carrion,
a coyote roadkill that survived winter
for this. To the west, craggy peaks
snag clouds that blur their edges,
brilliant white cornices dissolving into spray.
The river runs brown and gray, rising
toward spring torrent but not yet high enough
to scrub the boulders' icy crowns away.

Poem For Your Shoes

They remained in the front hall of my house
these two weeks, gathering heaviness

until I could barely lift them. I tried to hoist
the left shoe first and so unleashed

a plume of hot debris, Vesuvius raining
on a phalanx of scared people, hair and skin

afire. Of course I put it down and tried the right.
Into vast emptiness I spun, my breath disappearing

down the hollow's utter darkness.
I heard my own shoes in the closet

leap and clatter, running. I heard the shoes
of three thousand people do the same.

Someone said when we walk again it will be
barefoot like ancient men or mad

philosophers, crossing a desert's
rock and sand, our feet grown tough.

I am glad to return these shoes to you,
knowing you'll see in my strange dream

a poor attempt to find fear's edge and
tear it away, to name it so I can know it.

Forgive me. I could not walk a mile
and be in a safer place.

This Evening of War

Under great weight the aged elms
splinter and shred, high limbs
thick as a man's thigh fall to earth

in a spray of snow. The front yard
grows heaps of tangled wood,
sodden stump ends jagged and exposed.

There may never be peace again.
I am choked with sand in my dream
but awake to find an avalanche has

filled streets only tanks could cross.
This ice is chemical, winter's wasted
effort. Spring will never come.

Finally, sleep brings another dream—
neighbor boy dribbling a basketball home.
Suddenly, he's running from guns.

Tomorrow, I'll tug great branches
from drifts, break a thousand sticks
and cut the thick ones into hunks

to burn on long, cold nights.
I cannot face that task today, having seen
the teenaged soldier's panic as he

huddled in a shallow hole
scooped from ancient sand. I cannot
pray. The god evoked by enemies

and countrymen has gone away,
disgusted with his carnival turned
to a grotesque jig of gore and flames.

No song will save us. Let the snow
cover everything now, the jingo's giant truck
and the wretched overpass, hanging

half finished, a concrete and rebar gash
against the dawn. Having smelled blood,
crows are sure to cluster, a murder perched

in the fractured trees, calling names
of dead men in a language we don't know
but soon must learn.

Black Canyon Suite

1. Falcon, Tomichi Point

I would be a peregrine,
soaring, diving down again
on currents between canyon walls,
chasing down the canyon wren.

The rattlesnake, awakening,
will never hear the song I sing.
He of earth at last will fly,
clutched in talons, circling high.

River ribbons far below
rim rock spread with April snow.
Rockfalls slide past spires steep,
naming secrets I must keep.

From my eyrie, all I see,
rock and cloud, bush and tree,
scrub oak trees and piñon pine,
I will never call them mine.

Though into this canyon born,
on a high ledge, split and worn,
I'll pass my days above the wall
and die, and let my feathers fall.

I would be a peregrine,
soaring, diving down again
on currents between canyon walls,
chasing down the canyon wren.

2. Pegmatite Dikes: A Found Poem

In Precambrian times, molten rock
squeezed into fissures, minerals
crystallizing as it cooled, pale strands
binding dark rock together.
Mica, feldspar, garnet, quartz, a spur
jutting out as eons of wind and water
carved away the softer stone.

3. Devil's Lookout

Four buzzards cruise the rims,
red-fleshed faces and skulls,
confident as criminals
awaiting dusk. They would be as noble

as the eagle but for a dark love
of carrion—scavengers, not raptors.
Was winter long this year?
The Gunnison's once-frantic

spring gush, tamed now by dams,
sounds as but murmuring,
a lost song, a blue-green lyric
offered to the canyon walls.

4. Snowstorm, Rock Point

Finally, clouds break and it comes.
In the distance a white blur
sweeps down the thousand-foot face,
black rock alive with crazy whorls.

In the distance, a white blur.
Impassive monolith with stern crags,
black rock alive with crazy whorls
leans into winter's last kiss.

Impassive monolith with stern crags
gathers pebbles of frozen rain,
leans into winter's last kiss,
remembering summer, forgetting wind.

Gathering pebbles of frozen rain,
the river below hurries away,
remembering summer, forgetting wind.
Swollen already with runoff,

the river below hurries away
as snowbeads ping off my cheek and palm.
Swollen already with runoff,
green-brown Gunnison sings at sky.

Snow sweeps down the thousand-foot face,
slows and stops as clouds break.

5. Mating Swifts, Pulpit Rock

Rock dwellers,
air sailors,
white-throated and
swift enough
to earn your name.
Sometimes, though,
you're falcon's prey.
You dive as if
dying from flight,
then mate mid-air in
passion's spiral,
a death dance
conjuring life
between cliffs.

Lunch With Creeley

It's May, warm. Tender green
flares from a canopy
of cottonwoods,

branches dipping
as we drive beneath them,
across the Higgins Street Bridge

for lunch. The restaurant is
an old whorehouse,
the bricks in back

gone patchy gray. It overlooks
the river, and all the fish are women
leapt from windows winters

when the ice was thin.
We sit near the bar but he doesn't
order beer—

just a sandwich and a mug of tea
and he speaks of
Auburn prison,

where he read inmates' poems.
That's my home town, I say,
recalling the fortress

with badass gunners
peering through green glass,
prisoners themselves

in turrets atop high walls.
They closed my school once
when news of an escape

filled the radio waves. Even if a man
could scale a concrete slab
that tall and thick and slip

the gauntlet of frantic guards
firing at his back,
where would he go then?

Creeley says the hotel room
is comfortable and smiles
for the first time.

I hadn't written a poem in months,
he says, but when I walked
into that room,

saw brown grass sway
on the hill's incline, saw sun
flash on river shallows,

saw the shiver of new-fleshed trees,
it made me weep.
I had to sit down

and write.
He's got the poem
on a wrinkled page

and he reads it to me,
sitting there in the café
as the waitress

floats into view and
without interrupting his song,
leaves the check.

Elvis Comes Back

He stands before the supermarket tabloid rack
shaking his head back and forth, battered guitar
slung behind his shoulder on a strap, as if his hip
were about to jut the way it used to, as if he were done
playing his chords and was ready to sneer
and sing. Nobody notices Elvis

standing before the supermarket tabloid rack. His sullen face
is bloated still, and yet more pale. He's staring at *The Star*,
with its banner head above his photo:
ELVIS SIGHTED IN PISCATAWAY BY NEW JERSEY COP
Elvis shakes his head, knows he's never been
to Piscataway, not even since he died.

Elvis came back to complain about rap and D.J. Moe's
backbeat version of "Don't Be Cruel" and the use of
"Mystery Train" to sell sneakers on TV. Elvis came back
to put to rest all rumors he was a pervert,
that he liked his women sedated, comatose,
or fondling each other on the blind side of a one-way mirror.
Elvis wants to contradict the one who said she took him home

after finding him in a Vegas bar, too stoned to stand,
slurping a beer and humming "Love Me Tender."
He wants to have a word with the man
who gave him all those barbiturates. He wants to wear
his leather pants just one more time and slink up to
a microphone among a host of impersonators, cock his hip
and sling the rockabilly band into "Jailhouse Rock."

He knows he's not too old, he knows his comeback
could be comeback of the year. He only wants a little
justice in this world, some peace and some respect for the dead.
Elvis leaves the tabloid rack and ducks next door
into the closest pub, stands in front of the
juke box, fumbles in his pocket for a quarter.

Motorcycle Suite

1. *January*

I open the throttle on a
wind-whipped hill, dun slope
parched by a winter without snow.
Morning sun pours faintly down
and cold licks exposed skin.
There's no reason to ride in
midwinter, except for pure joy
and open road, the thrum of engine
huddling hot between thighs.
I cruise up a red rock canyon,
ledges so smooth I want to
lie down there to dream.
Cold air finds every gap—cuffs
boot tops, and collar. Spring
will surely come, warm afternoons
and light late into evening, but now,
the hag of winter hasn't cast aside
her cloak to show a mossy lee.
The foothills gather dark blues
in every ravine, hoarding frost.
I turn for home.

2. *April*

Last night's snowfall, heavy as regret,
bends the forsythia low, then melts
by noon. The streets turn clear and dry.
Wind swirls in all directions but
does not gust, feels nearly warm enough.

In this troubled spring, reservoirs shrink
to meager ponds, green slicks
that murmur *drought* to shrunken mud.
A thousand creatures whisper back the word.
The road curves past river's brown funk,

dividing the city's grime and gleam,
the low brick flats, the palatial towers,
chrome and glass plinths vying for sun.
This road leads out of spring
toward summer, yet all around me people
hunch in their cars as if scared,

listening to live reports, digitized blasts
of small arms fire, the cries of
mothers and fathers in far countries.
All they want is to drive on toward the
sun falling for the distant horizon, toward
familiar faces, no danger, home.

3. *August*

The first thing I see is a woman wearing
Medea's mask, standing in the middle
of the Interstate, arms frantic,
hot wind whipping long hair
about her head like black flames.
Brake lights flare and the few cars on this
desolate pavement cruise on through
high desert south of Raton. The rider
lies prone on the highway as
another man cuts away his pants
and he prays aloud in Spanish, crying *"¡Dios!"*
His forearms are shucked of skin,
elbow bones speckled with bits of rock.

A long way down the road
his cycle drips gas onto hot asphalt,
vapors wrinkling air. I hoist it upright,
shut off the fuel line, my hands
drenched. The clutch won't budge and
the back wheel is locked up. A woman
helps me drag the bike to the dirt.

"¡Dios!" again.

4. October

Blazing yellow cottonwoods
shimmer in chill morning wind.
I choke the engine to chase cold
out of the line. It's slow starting,
but rumbles once cylinders warm.
The sun's an imposter. Summer went south,
so I button down sleeves and the
neck of my jacket, close the helmet vents.
The heat from the engine
warms my legs. Who ever knows which
will be his last ride? As soon as
front tire meets street,
a gust whips round me a thousand
golden leaves swirling,
and I chase the fleeing vortex,
cutting turns close, my head full of
autumn poems and color because
I skipped work today. Screw 'em.
Sometimes, you just have to ride.

Observatory Park, Denver

Winter morning sun is a tepid salve
on night's cold burn, when stars
teased through the ground glow,

dim and not dimly aware of
the shining dome, its lid closed,
the old telescope's lens hooded.

Didn't the builders know
a century ago that this city would
sprawl and brighten, become visible

from space as a phosphor bloom,
luminous with dust sifted from
the hulls of prairie schooners?

Maybe tonight, phantom astronomers
will slip the padlocked doors and
turn the wheel again, the flange

parting to reveal meteors'
persistent trains, Neptune's green globe,
and the Seven Sisters, clustered

and whispering celestial secrets
amid the spinning, the burning,
the orbits, and the asteroids.

Elegy for Rosa

You confessed, finally, it wasn't aching feet
or tiredness in your bones that made you sit
at the front of the bus. You could have

trundled to a bench seat in the back. You had
energy enough for that, the world soon learned.
You told the driver no when he insisted that you

offer your seat to the man whose pale skin
was his ticket, and your voice shook loose
a crust of disgrace from the centuries,

shuddering back through the timber of slave ships,
rippling forward through the wombs of women,
through the windows of classrooms and offices,

flickering in flames of restaurant stoves,
bubbling up through water fountains and
greening the trees of neighborhoods where

children's laughter makes a new music.
How long did you sit before the cops arrived
to haul you out of your seat and off the bus?

When they did, into the vacuum whirled
the severed tongues of bigots, shackles
wet with blood, moans of mothers

whose children were stolen, the rage
of men whose wives were sold to rape.
Would that I had been on that bus,

a witness. My birth came a decade later,
after your work had begun to clear
the refuse away. Today, your death

reminds us we've more stones to roll
uphill, more seats to occupy and more
commands from fools to refuse.

Seacoast Suite

1. *Yaquina Bay, Summer Dawn*

This is the last view the two men had
as they left home: a gray, placid bay
swelling under the bridge, the casual

arcs of seagulls and the blown-back
cypress leaning forever into
Pacific wind soggy with mist.

The storm, burgeoning over the sea
like an accident, must have surprised
those fishermen there in their craft,

too far from land for a squawking radio
to reach and bring rescue in time.
Where they went down, no one knows.

No one else knows how cold the water
far beneath the surface. Somewhere
their bodies still swirl

in a sad ballet, limbs gesticulating
in the murk, a gesture for the sablefish
they meant to catch that now

mock their beckoning hands
from just beyond reach. Months
have passed and winter's storms are dreams

from which a woman wakes, sure
her son and husband will return.
She stands on the beach and turns

her face from the breakers, the sea
and sand and salt air
singing shanteys to her silence.

2. November at the Sea

They stand at the edge of the world
among great redwoods, talking of
summer past, of the chilling waters

frothed with whitecaps, of the way
wind blows mist across the cliff,
obscures the crooked path, the ferns

plunging up from forest loam,
a mist scented with sea foam and
the deep ache of seagulls' cries.

She may have cut her hair or changed her name.
He may not recognize her face,
a place he once belonged.

She may touch him as she once did
with fingers small as a child's,
straightening his ruffled hair, erasing

his memory of falling from cliff to beach,
landing amid driftwood and fleshy kelp,
swallowing back blood and bitterness.

They may walk together till pale light fades,
having understood truths and love's half-lies,
each word in the silence of goodbyes.

3. Bald Hills, Big Trees, Mad River

The highway has heaved and buckled,
as if soft. Two great birds, black

as your lost days, find grooves in the sky
and ride them lazily, bored with roadkill.

Dirt roads climb the impossible slopes of
mountains, reminders of a before time

when cedars and sequoia sempervirens
bristled in Pacific wind and rain.

Now clearcuts flow with mud until
only rock remains. The mad river below

spills over snags and boulders, pulls
the last of spring in a green rush

from high places. There are no
bits of bark in your mouth, there are no

slivers under your fingernails, not even
a smear of sap on your palm.

Drive on. You may look back some day
and see a blameless place, children

splashing in river shallows, the living
tower of a giant tree thrusting up

from the edge of a deep green pool,
its clear water more inviting than life.

None of this could survive in a canyon
forgotten by gods and found by men.

The sharp blades ripped wood
for houses where we live,

angry sons whose fathers cut
too much and left us these bald hills.

4. *Goodbye to the Dusky Seaside Sparrow*

You were not powerful like the condor with his
huge wings and beak a red half-moon,
his talons made for tearing.
Reports of your demise were not
exaggerated; with no mate remaining
you lived out what was left of life
somewhere in Florida, a captive,
imaginary females in the trees
beyond the window, their shrill calls
carried away on a breeze rustling
through palm fronds, shuddering down
bearded moss. There are no pastel eggs
in old nests cupping tropic sun.
The surf, the surf hushed you to sleep.
We build roads because we cannot fly
and never will. Even your frail wings
we cannot master, mysteries of
feather, bone, and air. Our asphalt slashes
through the marshes toward
exhaustion. Extinction has its privileges:
no need to feed the young
so hungry for the scavenged fish
or any scrap you zip up from your gut.
We've rearranged the species
all by accident. We meant to save
ourselves but we gnawed away ozone,

drained the aquifers, poured
concrete as though it would last.
Fossil fuels made some men rich,
while others split atoms like agates,
opening Hell's gates for poison blossoms.
It's evolution. With you goes the tiny fish
found only in one Texas spring,
and tomorrow a hundred others.
For now, hope hides in a burrow where
five wet pups slide from the womb
to join the Magic Pack, roaming south
through lands they once called home.

5. Toxicosis

tall palms whip the sky in L.A.
dull-thorned shrubs flank raised freeways
where billboard thighs drop hints of sweat
thrust up on stilts from cemetery turf
new V6 engines thrum and combust
rat-faced businessmen tensed in sedans
in gridlock, light with little rat hands
their cigarettes, their silhouettes
backlit in a syrup, quick eyes dart
parched, shot with blood
a radio huckster says something about
two for the price or else twice the amount
no going back to pale desert that once
sprawled from dunes to arroyo rims
where gargoyle coyotes perch and croon,
laugh like rogues when the freeway clogs
flutter stone wings from the Hollywood sign
city of segregate angelic wealth

a dusty brick mission two centuries past
a place where the Chumash once launched their canoes
now Dodgers, Lakers, Angels, Kings
draw exorbitant salaries, sport diamond rings
laugh at fans in the barrio, condo, ghetto
some day the Earth may open its maw
and suck down the Porsches, film studios, malls
the hovels, the banks, the homes of the stars,
snap them loose from their pipes, slough them to sea
scrub from its surface the tar and cement
shuffle the granules, try to erase
bilge brown film from San Gabriel's face
until such a time as it buckles and shrinks
until the Mojave creeps over the crest
and real estate values deflate and collapse
or mad conflagrations sterilize slopes
and giant tsunamis wash in, wash out
the gluttonous crush will consume and replay
and the tall palms will whip at the sky in LA

6. *Anacapa*

Lonely as an asteroid
tumbling through space
in a silent wind,
this island splits waves,

forms a seam in the blue.
Huge jellyfish snag and
die on the rocks,
great bags of shucked,

transparent skin,
splayed tendrils
glued to gritty sand.
Primal fear stays your hand.

You came this far
and cannot return
across a dangerous sea
where ships chase the sun.

Those things you constructed
you could lose on this island
where a tear is as salty
as the ocean it joins,

a seed that falls to
chalky cliffs cupping nests
of gulls and pelicans
that fold their wings and dive.

The coast you left behind
is now a mirage
below a moon
blurred in the mist.

You cannot fly
with the flying fish,
flicking their tails
on the surface, you cannot

come to live here,
carve your name in soft rock,
find fresh water or
trap the brilliant birds.

There is only time
to swim in the cove,
strange seaweed hands
clasping at feet and thighs

when you dive down
through pale green water,
through a forest of fronds
glowing with twilight.

I Will Not Argue With the Cucumber Plant

Brisk wind rustles the browning corn
as sun slides low in its autumn slant.
Strawberries bleed where heat once burned
this patch of soil to a garden turned.
On such a cool and lovely morn,
I will not argue with the cucumber plant

that beckons feebly from its trellis,
where once it spilled in June's profusion,
not so gaudy now after one chill night,
dripping and drooping in day's first light.
What do these mute green tendrils tell us
of immortality's illusion?

The queen of summer has taken her lover
and guides him toward her bed of leaves,
first fall from the elm and ash.
Across the still-green grass they dash
toward death. His bones the snow will cover
until fair spring, when in song she grieves

him forth, new-clad in robes of verdant cream,
bursting from scattered clods of earth.
Winter will be long, I know.
This is how the seasons go.
With summer's colors there to light my dream
I will cold nights abide, await rebirth.

The Defenseman's Lament

Papa was fast as a Saskatoon zephyr
blowing past in a blur of blades and color,
weaving past men who stood quaking like pines.
No one could catch him, touch him, or reach him,

blowing past in a blur of blades and color.
I tried to be like him, to match speed and grace,
but I never could catch him, touch him, or reach him.
He said, *"Son, use your size and play defense."*

I tried to be like him, to match speed and grace,
but the other boys beat me in race after race.
He said, *"Son, use your size and play defense."*
So I learned to skate backward and crash the corners,

crush the boys who beat me in race after race.
I grew bigger than Papa, great shoulders and thighs,
and I learned to skate backward, to crash the corners,
to poke with my stick and clear out the crease.

I grew bigger than Papa, great shoulders and thighs,
spent Saturday mornings on the small patch of pond,
learned to poke with my stick and clear out the crease,
and practiced my slapshot till I bled in my gloves.

I spent Saturday mornings on the small patch of pond,
with visions of Papa criss-crossing the ice,
and practiced my slapshot till I bled in my gloves,
till a cold wind made my eyes water and sting.

In dreams I still see him criss-crossing the ice.
In dreams he is lightning, sudden and blue,
a flash that can make your eyes water and sting,
a shot so hard it makes goalposts sing.

Now in games I see skaters flash sudden and blue,
and I hear the breath leave them when I take them down.
My shot is so hard it makes goalposts sing,
my face is so scarred it won't bleed any more.

I hear breath leave some skaters when I take them down
and I fight if I have to, so my knuckles are splayed,
my face is so scarred it won't bleed any more,
like the face that he wore and the hands that he used,

Papa, so fast, like a Saskatoon zephyr,
he blew through my life like he blew down the ice,
past the defensemen who stood quaking like pines,
and into that zone without any lines.

Highway Suite

1. Backroad Roadkill

What were these bodies
on the highway? There is no god
but asphalt, no heat like the sun

that burns backroads. There is no way
to avoid a bloody carcass
when cresting a hill.

When a bird whacks your grill,
vacation is over. The crow flies low
and dies against trucks carting

empty trailers north.
The crow mourns itself by
bearing black children.

2. Heart Mountain Elegy

I take wire-cutters from my belt,
snip a six-inch strip of
rusty barbed wire

from the forgotten coil
half-buried in granular dust.
At the sound of the cutting,

ten thousand ghosts rush up
from invisible barracks,
shapes shimmering as they

leap low sage and scatter among
great cottonwoods growing in the
groins of gullies between dun buttes.

The wind won't quit,
even for this fair spring noon.
It drags through branches

of a lone Russian olive that
struggles up from tumbled bricks
at the high chimney's base.

After the last family left,
government workers
tore down every shack

and spared only the
brick power plant and shabby
hospital to mark our shame.

Then wind erased the names:
Hideki, Atsuyo, Miamura.
The camp now lies under

fields of alfalfa watered by
ditches the prisoners dug.
The mountain above still wears its

stern face, inclines crossed by
shadows and pronghorn, washed
by sudden rains and long lost years.

3. At The Wheatfield, Gettysburg

Smooth stones stacked in rows, pocked
by bullets and draped with green-gray lichen—

this was the only cover under
hot July sun, emanating heat to match

the fear of desperate men on their bellies,
a scent that soaked every surface,

a residue centuries can't erase. Perimeter oaks
wear ancient ribbons of gnawed bark

Thirty feet above the earth to mark the rifles'
fusilade, mineé balls burrowing

deep into wood. What courage or foolishness
drives men over such a low stone wall

and toward a row of cannon, stocks red hot,
barrels stuffed with double canister?

There were lead shells big as melons meant to
snap off trees, send crowns crashing down

on men below. Outside the farm house
turned hospital, surgeons piled the limbs

in heaps. At night, men groaned from the field
for water, for a bullet to end their agony.

Bodies lay for days in July heat, forgotten
in Lee's retreat and Meade's sullen pursuit.

One soldier lay a century, bleached bones found
in a hidden glen by a boy. Now, stones mark where

regiments stood, where men fell and blood spilled,
and soft rain rinses what can never come clean.

4. Lost in Nevada With You

A handful of desert sage, the green blush
of June on the slopes, the healed moon
rising over a ridge—all this was here

Twenty years ago, when your skin was
the first landscape I crossed
surviving on water alone.

Now years have gathered
in your hair, silver veins
spiraling through red earth, awaiting

the shuffle of miners' feet measuring
an age and an age, fathers and sons,
as generations turn.

I would go anywhere with you
and remember it well, the path
we took and all the stones and every

hawk rising on currents above us.
This time, we travel with our children
who test—but don't yet cross—

a green river soon to carry them
far away. Let us look
deeply at them; drink like this was

the last draught taken from a
vanishing stream. I will go on with you.
Don't fear, here is my hand.

5. Inferno Casino

A lost soul pulls a lever with desultory hand.
Coins clang in the empty hall of dreams
she once inhabited but now only haunts.

See the waitress place the weak gin and tonic
near her elbow and retreat, afraid the
melting hair and pale skin is contagious,

afraid the awful sounds of a thousand birds
battering the thick glass of her stare
may soon break free and rampage.

Casino lights hum in a cigarette haze
and a man teeters near the cashier's kiosk,
hoping to cash in his misery chips.

The carpet's molten flow is a bad joke
beneath beat boots. Winter sun paints
colors on the stones beyond town and will

blind them when they emerge, broken,
unsure just what they left behind in those
seven levels of desperate gamblers, whores,

chain-smoking matrons who escaped Dallas
to stumble through ersatz damnation
and stand before the great volcano

spewing its magma of coins. The gondolier
on the phony canal is a boy from Topeka
who fled his father's hate to pole a punt

through this meta-Venice for miserable tips.
Dante deals blackjack at a crowded table.
The man at his shoulder cries, *"Almost, almost!"*

then turns to descend to his destiny—
washing forever the sheets stained with faces.
Outside, a desert wind that once bore sage and snow

pushes trash along the avenue.
A shopping cart lady in her silent
grief and rage bends low into the gust.

6. The Trains of Pasco, Washington

The trains of Pasco, Washington,
come from afar, Chicago or Seattle.
You need not press an ear to the
steel strip; their approach is measured
as gently, tumblers shiver upon the
motel sink and windows vibrate
in their panes though the trains
are still miles away.
When finally they rumble through town,
the cat leaps to the windowsill, arches
her back and the dog barks softly
once, then lies back down.
The tumbler skitters to the
edge of the sink, falls and shatters.

The trains of Pasco, Washington,
are surely going somewhere
when they leave so empty.
Locals know the cars' cargo—
old reactors broken in bits,
bagged contaminated suits,
shirts and gloves and rubber boots
some father wore—another town's
dark treasure now is theirs. They know
blue sage glows just the same
both sides of the perimeter fence
that never contained a loose neutron.
They know spent fuel rods point from
core to star, that only .07
cancer deaths occur each year in town.
They know the jackrabbits'
overlong ears are not accidents.

And when the trains have shuddered away,
sleep comes to the streetlamp motel night.
The cat creeps across the headboard, whispers
forgive them all the ugliness,
forget the big river and threatening hills,
forget the buzzards circling
below the curl of damaged clouds,
forget the man in the parking lot
who watched the suitcase in your hand
as if it were full of secret plans.
The cat says go on back to sleep,
but take me with you
when you leave.

7. Why the S.F. Bus Station Seemed Lonely
One Busy August Morning

You might think the man
in the blue ball cap
would talk to someone,

explain his enormous grief
over having to wear such pants,
too small, smeared with grease,

or those white vinyl shoes,
stark on the twig-ends
of his legs.

Instead he just talks to himself,
mumbling and biting off words,
gristle from a mind gone to bone.

On the filthy tile floor a family huddles
because there are no seats.
Their boxes read BANGKOK.

Mother wipes the crumbs
from her little girl's face, speaks
in her strange, musical tongue

and folds herself so small she seems
no more than a child herself.
Across the room, an argument erupts,

a man shouting *"faggot, faggot!"*
at no one in particular,
wildly waving his hands.

Outside the windows,
dozens of pigeons huddle
on a narrow ledge,

wet, gray towels thrown down,
only a trembling feather to
betray the disguise.

The woman near the garbage can
begins to cry and turns
to hide her face.

Buses line up
beyond the double doors
but no one boards.

Perhaps no one will ever leave
or arrive. The birds may never fly
from the ledge, their feathers finally

detaching and blowing away
down streets toward the bay, leaving
small heaps of thin hollow bones to bleach

slowly in weak sun.
Perhaps the family is returning to,
not arriving from, Bangkok.

Perhaps we are all refugees
this morning, even the man
bleating into his cell phone,

digital voice radiating its prayer
down the canyon of gray towers,
their crowns faint in the fog.

8. *At the Discount Store in Durango, Colorado*

Across this white tile prairie
the herd roams, wide-eyed antelope

exploring the aisles,
the vertical stripes of their shirts

hugging breasts tightly
to their ribs, their shoulders brushing

against racks of clothes
in departments of men, boys, girls,

where fantastic plastic gadgets
for kitchen and bath

share space with cheap pillows,
promises of sleep sifting

out of the seams to float above the
sale signs on cotton sheets.

Everyone knows the parking lot
sags from the weight of cars

loaded down by debt, dreams
badly stuffed in the trunks

so their shoeless legs protrude.
Everyone knows the store closes

before all urges are exhausted.
This does not stop these women

from coming, delicately lifting
from shelves the bowls and toys

they didn't plan to buy
but now know that they will,

despite the impatience of husbands
slouching behind them, hands

probing pocket holes, bootheels
clacking down narrow corridors.

They see through the green storefront glass
all the rest of the world

to which they soon must return
with twelve dollars less, navigating stoplights,

heading for homes and the soft swish
of shopping bags in the hall.

How I Swam to the Bottom of the Ocean

I did it on a dare; my friend was smug
about my inevitable failure, saying
"You know you'll never make it." So I
stripped my clothes right there, left
pants and shirt and shoes right on the sand
and waded into surf, the frigid water
snapping my testicles to attention.
I wanted to not look back but I was
weak at that moment and so I turned,
looked over my shoulder to where he stood,
arms folded, grin on his face. He waved
a little wave as if to say *"Go on,
I will comfort your woman."*
Then came the moment of truth. The water
swelled and my body left the firm
footing beneath; I was afloat.
I breathed my deepest breath and dove
down, down, down, salt stinging my eyes
when I opened them to measure the
fading light. I thought I'd see
sharks but at first it was only
tangled mats of seaweed clinging
to my arms and neck. *Oh, for a machete,*
I thought. Just then, a yellow fish
kissed my forehead. In shock,
I opened my mouth and out came
all my air. But the kiss had freed me.
I could breath the water like she could
breathe the water, gills suddenly
flapping beneath my jaw. The pressure
in my ears subsided. I propelled myself
down to where organic bits swirled

as dust motes float in sun shafts
of abandoned rooms. Shapes emerged
to left and right, coarse heaps of rock.
The deeper I went the darker it got,
until I swam not by sight but by feel,
seeking thicker water, colder, more black.
Things brushed along my sides, smooth
and muscled creatures, checking out
my size and shape. I felt welcome,
unafraid. Finally, I found the ocean floor,
silt so soft I burrowed in a foot, my face
embraced by a cool palm.
I would have stayed, I swear, but knew
my friend was already on his
cell phone, calling the coroner,
arranging for flowers to be delivered
to a church I never visit. Coming up
was harder; the light above
flowed against me like current,
buffeting me with all the things
to which I would return: my desk,
my car, tax forms, a pending
prostate exam. Still, that's where I
belonged. When I emerged again,
it was night in a foreign land.

Regarding the Budget Cuts: A Found Poem

I thought it would be helpful
to share information on the process
and the factors used
in determining which people
and programs
would be adversely affected by the
budget cuts this year.

This spreadsheet was created for the
quantitative analysis done in
evaluating the personnel decisions
that I made in light of
the budget cuts this year.

The factors in this analysis
are similar to the ones from
last year when
all other programs
were involved in a
further analysis of
qualitative factors
relevant to personnel decisions
in those departments.

I did not set parameters
regarding the qualitative information.
Factors included the
extent of new initiatives, the
future outlook for success, the
starting salaries, the
partnerships created or dissolved,
etc.

I then made decisions without regard
to the detrimental actions
that would occur.

If you have further questions please
speak with your supervisor.
I do not think it is helpful
to make this information
public.

Suite of Seasons

1. *The Bird at the Foot of the Bed*

I must admit, at first
the stuffed crow scared me,
perched as he is on the rail
at the foot of the bed, a reminder

that waking up is temporary
and we best not forget
one chill morning that joke
will finally be funny

but we won't be able to laugh.
Night falls slowly, boulders
on the hill growing gray beards
in the half light,

lips mumbling
in bass tones of the plume
drifting from this cabin's
chimney pipe up canyon walls,

the canyon itself a clock I could
mark time upon, a shaft of sunlight here,
a shadow there for solstice, equinox,
all things slow and regular.

We ourselves are just electric sparks
that take brief residence, rebuild
the walls and roof, dream
tremulous dreams beneath the gaze

of the grinning crow, wake to stir
the ashes in the stove,
turn out the lights, replace the locks,
and then we're gone.

2. Red Moon

January's grass wears a sheath of frost
so thin the touch of fingers melts the white away.
Wind scours the hogback, swishes past
pines that lurk in the shadows, chilling both
man and dog out for a late night walk.
Totality comes slowly, the sliding disk of black
an adumbration, the dragon of winter
biting a distant orb. Finally, we've escaped
the lights of town. I lie down.
The dog, unsure, settles nearby
but pays no attention to the moon, its upper edge
a crescent of white hot light
painted on a swollen stone. Faint redness
creeps across the dimming surface until spikes
of light shoot out from the shaded diamond. Then,
darkness wins. The red moon hangs suspended
in its arc as cops arrive and chase us from the park.

3. Standing in the Street

You're standing in the street at night,
winter haze obscuring the image now.
No one has ever traveled in time, caught
his own future through a window.

Your son and daughter are singing, playing
rough songs on the living room piano,
ageless in motion, at an apex, strong,
and you would teach them to be fearless

if such a thing were wise or possible.
This night will last a few minutes less
than the next, and yet the inexpressible
beauty of this frame you cannot lose.

4. Girls' Soccer Practice, February

Voices rise above the field, laughter
and shrieks of excitement.
Long-legged, they cross the turf

gold-brown, with spring's hint of green
underneath, patches of snowcrust
hiding on hill's north slope.

This sun, gentle and welcome,
will scorch by May, its heat
no longer chased by breezes

off the peaks. The goalposts
bear no nets, only streaks of rust
down white paint. The lines

on the field are last year's lines,
faint but visible. The games
are still far off. For now

practice on an chilly day
beats books and bad TV,
being home alone, and boys.

5. Rondeau for Late Winter

Dusk comes down the hills, cold silent shapes
backlit by frail sun. Yesterday I closed the drapes
on morning light I'd welcome now, anything
that gives heat; my bones can't wait for spring.
I watch as one more winter day escapes.

Feel the wind come howling, see how it scrapes
at the field's snow crust, how it wraps
around tree trunks, lifts the high crow's wing.
Dusk comes down the hills;

The sun's an addiction, worst when night lays ropes
of stars across sky; a familiar scupper dips
into the black. Chill shrinks the ring
on my finger and then the finger, too. I sing
for early dawn, notes lost on silent shapes,
as dusk comes down the hills.

6. Poem for Baseball Season

March sun, low and bright,
floods the field, grass brown
but for a green swath behind short

where years of dying pop flies fell,
left soil fertile. Now at home plate,
young men gather, shirts so blue the sky

goes dark for a moment. Every leather glove
is oiled and bats still faintly ring with
last year's doubles and triples.

Blackbirds in bare trees call the game
and mispronounce each name, sure
the ball will never reach their roosts.

The chain link fence glows silver
and the dugout fills with voices
not heard since September's last inning

when a deep shot to left won it all.
This first day of practice,
before the first pitch is hurled,

every swing is yet to come, each slide
awaits the umpire's gruff call.
No games yet are lost or won,

and no one has struck out
with the tying run on third.
A bat's crack turns loose spring,

the ball landing soft on outfield grass
as the second baseman waves his arm
and the runner tries for two.

7. *Harbinger, Past Midnight*

While she sleeps, sleet taps the glass,
half hail, half rain, melting or freezing.
She breathes in slow circles, far from the surface.
Night flows through her empty rooms,

half hail, half rain, melting or freezing.
A winter-spring waterfall spills down the dark.
Night flows through her empty rooms,
awash in cool moisture, quiet and weightless.

A winter-spring waterfall spills down the dark,
to spark the bloom of bulbs in dirt,
awash in cool moisture, quiet and weightless,
awaiting the warmth of sun upon earth.

The spark and bloom of bulbs in the dirt—
she imagines them moving in still frigid sod,
awaiting the warmth of sun upon earth.
Sleet falls and gathers, small stones of ice.

She imagines what moves in still frigid sod,
the bright bliss of her dream splashed with color.
Sleet falls and gathers, small stones of ice
spatter upon the window above her.

Bright bliss of her dream, splashed in color
as the night sky inhales, fading away.
The last sleet spatters the window above her,
then silence returns, an unusual calm.

The night sky inhales, fading away
as stormclouds loosen a slow spring dawn.
Then silence returns, an unusual calm
in thunderclap's vacated concentric circles.

The night sky exhales, fading away
as stormclouds loosen a slow spring dawn,
and while she sleeps, sleet taps the glass
and she breathes in slow circles, close to the surface.

8. *Black Calendar*

crow in winter
on a tilted fencepost

a windless stretch
of crusted snow

roost in a tree
within circling trees

the perimeter of
a holy place

crow in spring
a grip on hard buds

rain rolls off you
who absorb nothing

one caw for loneliness
one for the babies

born this year
one caw for the disappeared

crow in summer
pecking the opossum's

carcass, a scavenger
with two gold eyes

fleeing our bad dreams
in a thick flash of wings

when the hot sun comes
no shade to be found

crow in autumn
when dead plants talk

sunflowers, cornstalks
hold brown leaves contorted

and the first frost forms
on everything but you

marking the sky
for holes to fly through

9. The Road Looks Like Rapids and the
Hail Sounds Like Applause

At two o'clock, black rainclouds heap up
north of town, readying to pour forth
their load of stones onto alfalfa farms
bisected by rural roads, kicked and penetrated
by the loaded ends of last week's
funnel clouds. Soon the wind slows down
and stops, the air so moist and cool that
children stand among castles of dirt
and lift their chins, deep breathing
the salt perfume of a coming storm.
Cottonwood leaves above them curl
the spades of their pale undersides
and crows, ecstatic and terrified, lurch
on the limbs, their rough, hacking calls
the only sound in the darkening afternoon
until a mother, one foot holding screen door ajar,
lets her thin, nervous voice unspool
and the children run squealing for home,
first drops wetting their flaxen hair.
Suddenly, balls of ice begin percussion
on the pavement and hoods of cars,
a staccato chorus pinging, then thrumming
as larger stones pour down, a sound like the
frenzied slapping of ten thousand hands
that rises, peaks, and fades.
Finishing rain carves braided channels
through mats of ice, rivulets laden with a
cargo of white spheres spill into ditches
as the downpour turns to drizzle lit by
ochre light, hushed by mumbling thunder.

10. Sonnet for a Girl Playing Violin
on the Porch at Autumn's Approach

At first, the sound of trucks is all I hear,
the rumbling of a hundred city streets.
But underneath the hum a thin strand greets
my ears, a whispering that trills, that calls me near.
The wind tugs at the highest notes and blurs
the deepest runs until they seem to slide
away. I wait for melody to ride
again above the barking of the curs
concealed behind a hedge. I will not clap
my hands when your last strains fade into night.
Somehow applause would seem more wrong than right.
Instead, I'll let the autumn silence wrap
its cooling comfort round this evening scene,
your music dissipating down the green.

11. Summertail

A quiet song, the wind through stalks,
sways branches where the magpie walks.

Vanilla sun paints Silver Lace,
spreads yellow warmth upon your face.

No harsh rebukes from tongues of birds
can reach you now, you know the words

they squawk and shriek are nothing new,
their accusations aren't of you.

The longtail's parting cruel remark
dissolves to dust, blows past the park.

The cricket scratches slower now,
as red fruit bends the browning bough.

Summer never meant to stay,
no matter what the songbirds say,

no matter how pale tendrils twist,
reach one last time for what they wish.

The Arc of War

The bomb blew off a father's hand
and left it lying palm-up in the sand.
The blast that shook the desert night
was born of and died back to hate.
One finger wore a wedding band

that will not fit upon a stump. A wound
cannot caress away cares, strand by strand,
from her weary brow, nor hold her tight.
The bomb blew off

the hand that cups an infant, seals a bond
reforged since time began, in every land,
when a new life enters sunlight.
Each day, the hand that guides a child right
from wrong will be missed. So now, understand
what the bomb blew off.

Curfew

Nearly six feet tall, lean
as a longbowman's arrow,
he aims at his future,
reluctant to fly the bow.

All afternoon, dry snow smoothed
coarse hills to softness, pressed
the roofs of houses, pulled
blue smoke from chimneys. Dark

came early, a solstice kiss
like the last one you receive.
He dressed too spare for winter,
hands nervous as starved birds,

and looked in the mirror
a dozen times, eyes combing
his silhouette to make sure
he had not yet vanished.

I watched, statue of a father
in a village plaza, condemned
to witness the generations
passing to wars, to shores,

to mile-deep mines,
to the arms of their own children.
He paused at the door, expectant:
Midnight, I said.

City Suite

1. A Backpack Full of Glass

I want to make a window, she said,
something brilliant, blood red swaths
and hot yellow curls, a liquid array
of color and motion.

The only problem was
getting the glass home
on the motorcycle so I said,
Grab that backpack, the one we used

for camping down at Big Sur, and she said,
You want me to wear that
when it's full of glass, while we drive
down those crazy streets?

What if I fall on my ass, what then?
But finally she agreed and we got aboard
that tiny Honda street machine,
and cruised east on San Francisco streets,

up and down and up again, banking
on curved lanes in bright sun
and cold air, her arms hugging my ribs
tightly, her hair streaming

in my rear view mirrors.
We cruised up Potrero Hill,
and stopped to view in silence
Oakland across the bay,

the bridge's gray steel
set like the lines of solder
on the window she'd build, blue-green water
trapped in the spaces.

In the stained glass shop a woman
in a frayed apron pulled sheets
from tall wooden bins.
I remember how she handled those

transparent plates, how she scored them
with the knife, then tapped them so they
separated with a click,
their textures roped or bubbled

or smooth as still water.
Then carefully she wrapped each sheet
in newspaper, taping the corners
and stacking them on the table.

And when we began to load them into
the oversized pack the woman said,
Hold on, that just won't do.
I think I've got a box.

I said, *Well, thanks, but see*
we're on that bike, and I pointed
out through the clear panes
of her shoproom front

to our motorcycle, leaning into
the slope of the leaning street.
I could tell she thought we were nuts,
but we'd paid for the glass and now

it was ours. I noticed
as we pulled away,
she came to the door
just to see us go.

And that's how it went
the two of us up and down and up
the hills, reversing our route,
though more slowly this time,

the sun on a straight horizontal shot
into the confines of my helmet,
light sinking into the Pacific,
and she held on to me

tighter than she ever had
or ever has since, trusting me
almost entirely,
biting back her fear,

stoplights changing,
the engine straining,
and sheets of glass, their colors hidden,
vibrating against her spine.

2. Little Dry Creek

February sun, weak as a bad suggestion,
couldn't melt the film of ice today, pocked
by stones wild boys threw, marked with sigils of
twigs and leaves, with the last wishes of
suicides who gave up on spring. Tonight,

fresh snow will hide mud and weeds
for morning's debut when furious commuters
race across the bridge, the brown exhaust

from thousands sinking into soil.
Once, a woman squatted on those banks

to wash her hands and face, her baby asleep
in a patch of sun spread across rock.
No foam cups floated past, no rusted
supermarket buggy protruded
from the snag of cottonwood limbs.

The same creek twists now down its course
toward the Platte, wicked and rank.
The geese, the great blue herons, the few
pathetic trout carry on, dull with impending
death, remembering water cool and clear.

3. Man on the Bus Bench, 6 A.M.

Elms twist in gusts of
winter wind, losing last leaves,
and still you sleep in your

crib of glass beside derelict
brick buildings. Does any dream shuffle
down an alley in your head,

wrapped in its greasy wool cap?
What bed could reject
such tired bones?

Will you ever really wake? I know
you own this street and I trespass
as I step just out of reach, heading

toward my errands, collar turned against
cold wind, shoes scuffing quickly
past your fetal frame.

4. The Angry Man Eats Lunch Alone

All morning, I watched the traffic pile up
at the stoplight below
and later, I watched finches fight
a terrible November wind
to reach nests on my window ledge.
I know someone is dying somewhere
this morning, struggling to breathe
in a sunny room,
speechless, staring into the eyes
of his aged love, whose hand he grips
so tight with final strength
the last thing they share is pain.
You can judge me however you wish.
I will never learn to forget this. I'm like
a hungry child in bed,
unable to sleep, headlights
flashing across the torn paper
on the walls of my chilly room. I will wait
to grow more powerful. I will remember
whose teeth were black with lies.

5. Summer Comes to the Dry Lake

Ducks huddle at the center
of a paltry pool rimmed by a
wide ring of pale, cracked mud.

The weather is yet to turn
hot; today, a mass of gray clouds
diffuses sun and a chill breeze

serves as spring's goodbye.
April's scattered rains could not
fill up the lake. June sun

will bake it dry, every ash
and cottonwood will lean
toward the shallow, shrinking

patch of foul sludge
marking the bowl's low point.
It's what this town deserves,

though if I could I'd spare the birds
just now resting, their chatter
filling the yellow-green branches.

The old farm on the far side
is now a museum, safe from drought.
A hundred years ago

a man stood on that bank
and knew despair, the earth
turned in neat rows behind him and

awaiting seed, soon to come,
and rain that never would.
I'm waving to his ghost.

6. *Gasping for Breath*

It's late, maybe midnight when I
pull up to a stoplight
on a lonely street—industrial zone,
barrels of chemicals leaning into
old chain link and the sick moon
shining dull and pathetic through
November chill. I ought to be home,
I think, in my bed with a thick
blanket and her body for heat,
I ought to be off this street. Just then
a car pulls up next to mine
and stops. It's listing to one side,
a boat with its bilge full of water.
Bands of jagged rust arc above
bald tires and a heap of trash
spills over back seats. I gaze across
to the driver—a huge man
crammed in a tiny front seat, smoking—
but no, it's not a cigarette, it's a tube
wrapped across his upper lip,
secured around his ears.
His body pulls back, mouth open
as he gasps for breath, and gasps again
and again. It's horrible to watch, I
don't want to watch, but the light's red and
I can't drive away. He's sucking air
like great draughts of water, pulling
at the darkness, breath by breath,
never enough, I can tell from his face,
and the next thing I know I'm breathing
with him, for him, moving as he does,
mouth open and pulling back.

I'm so grateful when the light
turns green and his beat craft
lurches off, tailpipe spitting condensation;
I turn my car around and head for home.

7. *Snowfall, Suburbia*

The shrubs are hunched, cold cupcakes with dark rims
near the ground still showing green. Locust trees,
elms, cottonwoods that dared the night to freeze,
stand bowed, snow sloughing now and then from limbs,
their snapped ones lying scattered on the lawn.
No one thought a quiet suburban street
could fall more silent still. Snow turned the heat
of orange sun to gray before the dawn
filled up the blue and pale balloon of sky
with breath. Lights ping on in the neighbor's house,
gold stains spill on symetrical yard, loose
in a perimeter where snowmen fly,
stick arms outstretched, rock eyes and pebble grins
beneath the sagging wires in thick white skins.

8. *The Workers Down Below*

They seem, from twenty-one stories high,
too small to build a thing as grand
as a hotel. Look how slowly

they cross the concrete slab, carting
long strands of rebar on their shoulders
like half-cooked spaghetti.

One man sits atop the crane
in his little box, working the shafts
precisely so the enormous bucket

full of wet aggregate swings in slow motion
out over the busy street. But it's illusion—
the funnel end drops right into

the gaping form near a worker who waits
with his arms upraised, not in worship
but to signal *down*.

They work together without words,
coordinating motion in
true cooperation, nothing wasted.

Their bright plaid shirts suggest
a uniform, each hard hat like
a carapace. The overcoated foreman

weaves among the heaps of scrap,
a scroll of blueprints in his hand,
and two men follow. Soon

December dusk will claim remaining light
and workers grasping coolers
and spare coats will file out.

The operator will begin his long descent
down the narrow ladder, thinking
of arrival home, of lighted windows

beckoning, of the small arms of his children
reaching to embrace him,
a return to things quiet, soft, and warm.

9. *Walking to Manhattan*

August haze yellow with late sun
coats the leaves of maples, mimosas,
the great split rocks past which Washington
beat his retreat to the Delaware
as Howe lay wine-slick in Manhattan,
when streets were wide green swales and
fox and bear roamed the Pallisades.
Now the hills are house-heavy, the breezes are
part wind, part Wall Street bleating.
New immigrants are Korean, not Dutch,
though the Hudson still churns brown,
salt water swirling with fresh. The bridge
from Ft. Lee hums with automobiles
hurtling home from the city
gleaming with the day's last light.

10. *Sitting in My Car in the Rain*

Windshield wiper's bent metal
screeches on glass with each pass.
At least this rain will wash away
the birdshit, gray grease, seed pods
of the elms. I cut the engine.
A quiet comfort: slow spattering.
People, houses, trees outside
swirl on liquid surfaces,
suddenly beautiful again. Forget
wars and wars and wars. I can't hate
the world, though tonight I wish I could.

Ghazal for a Murdered Poet

for Nadia Anjuman, November 8, 2005

This morning when I heard, I looked in your eyes to find words,
hoping, though we speak different tongues, I might find words.

But those I found said only they discovered you too late,
bleeding on the floor, though they tried to find words.

Your husband said he beat you with his hands. He won't
allow an autopsy, afraid the doctors' hands might find words

to accuse him, written there in your blood, as a poem.
When his own last breath comes, may he sigh and find no words.

This evening, I watch rising hawks, turning under faint stars
in slow, distant circles and there, for you, I find words.

Coming Down the Mountain

I stood on the slope of the mountain amid
a field of gold flakes fluttering
in cold wind. I would tell you more,

I would, but words, you know,
they fail. Still, that's what I have—
ice, rock, knife-edge ridges,

peaks, couloirs, cliffs, and saddles.
I looked at the mountain and knew
I would ascend more slowly

than once I did, catching a breath of pine
and savoring oxygen.
I have chosen all my paths, good or ill,

no long falls but there were moments I clung
to sheer walls, toes in the cracks, afraid.
I looked at the mountain and saw myself,

the lesson of years teaching my eyes.
Now fewer paths open, green ones, the
coming down through meadows—knowing.

Albion Suite

1. *The Lonely Hills of Rhiwddolion*

On a day between rains I walk
Welsh ferns and gorse, oak and yew
never at rest in surging wind.

I bury a thousand bad days
under the Roman road,
Sarn Helen echoing weary steps.

Snowdon's slopes hide beneath
gray clouds. Sheep, suspicious
and slow, retreat as I approach,

but for one lamb sleeping, face
pressed into heather. *We're lost
in our past*, the old man said,

sitting in the cathedral's shade,
his eighty years measuring
but one of a dozen marks on the

sandstone arch guarded by a gargoyle—
farm wife forever screaming at us
to remember the Black Death.

That past recedes and so do I,
a pebble cast in the stream,
my bones polished by the breath of owls,

these poems perishing into pages
and pages into crumbling dust,
pathetic as slabs on the Abbey floor

once grandly carved—*Beneath this stone*
lie the remains of Robert—the rest
worn smooth by penitents' shoes.

I may return or never return.
The grass will keep my secrets safe,
the mossy limbs of the oaks

will fall into the shallow pool,
and the stone houses will fold
back into hillocks of stone.

2. Dolwyddelan

One summer's day in early June
we came through Conwy's vale alone
among scudding clouds,
escaping the crowds
through Welsh fern, well wind-blown

all along Gwyddelan's meadow.
Sun blazed bright, cast clean-edge shadow
on gorse and sheep-sheared
turf, and as we neared
where they fed, O they feared

and fled. A boy played near the barn
with his puppy, his pant-cuffs worn,
barefoot, face smudged, eyes
shining, chased his prize
toward the tarn near the rise

of rock on which the castle stood
these centuries since it withstood
ferocious attack
arrow-flight and axe-hack,
stone once good, now a wrack

of curtain wall around towers,
one keep tall, one crushed by powers
of time and disuse
rather than abuse.
White flowers now a truce

offered to dead Welshmen whose blood
once turned the earth here into mud.
Those blooms my feet trod
beneath Moel Siabod,
dreams a flood, words so odd

riffling my brains like a wind gust
through branches. A visitor, I just
wanted to witness
history, sightless
though I must be, witless

in a foreign land, and too late
to join with Llywelyn the Great
defending the pass
from Normans en masse.
Not my fate—galloglass.

So I climbed to the battlements'
crennelations, where I could sense
what Welsh princes knew,
finding it's still true:
eloquence, an era's due.

3. Churchyard Graves, Oxford

Stone melts slowly, wind working
smooth the clean lines of glyphs.
Date of death dissolves,
names rubbed away by
indifferent seasons' freeze and thaw.
The graves make of grass an
undulation in the forgotten square,
wretched slabs leaning
into eternity, pointing toward
the gate through which passed,
decades ago, the last known relative.
The only flowers here have come
from seeds on breezes, the only songs
from the throats of birds, and no tears
drop, just eroding rain.

Mr. James Waugh, your stone
sarcophagus makes a fine seat
here in the shade where I sit
to eat my lunch, away from exhaust
and the noise of history.
Perhaps no flesh has been nearer
your folded bones than mine
for many years, though alas,
it is only my ass. I've left no trash.
I wrote this poem, which too shall pass.

4. *Kenny the Paver*

In Talbot's Pub, Richmond town,
I met a man whose hands were
roughened by stone and mortar,
wild eyes blue as dawn, hair a nest of
tangles, teeth gapped in a grin
borrowed from a jester.
I bought him an ale; he bought me three
and rolled me cigarettes
which I smoked, though I do not smoke.
I clung to the edge of his
northern dialect, missing more words
than I caught. *Aye, a Yank then,*
he said, nodding as though I were
running from the law. *Don't quaff
that stoof*—he touched a tap handle—
*Old Peculier—turns tourists into
fairy folk,* he said with a wink.
We drank safer draughts, warm, sweet,
and he spoke nonsense woven with wisdom
as June dusk spilled through
four-square panes, washing the
dark oak tables and bar, casting
pale light down narrow lanes
all bending toward the market square,
where once a rebel priest was hung,
where thieves were whipped or worse.
They built the castle on Red Hill, he said,
a Norman fortress to guard the River Swale.
Masons, carvers, craftsmen came, fresh from
raising other walls—some never left.
Fifty generations later, Kenny
paves the courtyards of small homes
clinging to flanks of the hill beneath

crumbling curtain walls, only the keep
still whole and proud. I left him there
at the bar among drunken friends,
shook his hand and felt fingers
blunt and coarse, strong enough to
wedge rock and lift great weight.
Tomorrow night then, he said,
but he never came. Still, his smile was
so broad it crossed this ocean
and came home with me forever.

5. Little Girl's Coins

True abandon, a spring morning,
cool breezes polishing cobbles

of a narrow lane, Finkle Street.
She chases her friend,

bag swinging from wrist, auburn
locks streaming, laughter

streaming, and then the tinkling
of penny and two-penny coins

in an arc across stones.
For a long moment she stands,

eyes wide, taking in the
coppers spinning about her. Then

her eyes meet mine. I smile,
stoop, and gather coins,

dropping them in twos and threes
into her outstretched palms.

6. *On the Banks of the River Swale*

It's birdsong, the trill of wrens
blended into beeches and elms,
that coaxes this old river

once more past the crumbling castle,
sunlight surging, shadow rolling
over water and rounded rock.

I catch morning's end note
on this bank, guarded by green
sentinels, footsteps smothered

by the river's soft shush.
The day can wait, as it did
for some poor farmer centuries past,

who sought this stone seat,
this eddying sun and shade,
to cool his feet in the Swale

and leave the grain to grow.
They say workers unearthed
a handful of Roman coins

along this bank, a tin plate with
an etched sobriquet, like those
cast into Minerva's bath,

heavy enough to sink so a
conqueror's curse could not return
to trouble the caster's hand.

Today the only curse is the jet
splitting the sky, invisible
by the time its cry cuts through.

So another stone falls from the
castle's keep, another age turns
and another, and the river flows.

7. Bagden Wood, Sunrise

Only the meadow is lit this early,
yellow-green swatch between ash
and beech trees. Nuthatches trill,

invisible on their forest perches, songs
crosscut by the rook's harsh rebuke
and the mad rooster's cackle.

A great dragon undulates
through the hedge, guarding passage
to Bagden Wood where the fox's den

hides five pups born to scout this
bounded paradise for
rabbits, mice, and even a

wayward lamb, resting in the
shade of a great red oak,
regal in the field of ryegrass.

8. Kent Barrow

They chose this hill because the wild barley grew
on grades that undulate toward tomorrow
and from the valleys between, the eye flows true
over curves that conjure a woman. Here, sorrow
over death is but a thing to borrow

and give back when joy comes again in spring.
Five thousand years, and sun still paints slopes
they crossed with the dead. I hear them sing
low songs, fifty men dragging with crude ropes
great sarcen stones, Grey-wethers, in hopes

the soul might rest remembered in a tomb
bought with living labour. I climb that hill
on a June evening, pass the portal to a room
inside the tumulus, lintel stone letting light spill
beneath, earth swallowing me and my will.

9. London Bridge, Dawn

Flotsam reveals the river's flow,
away from here, as rivers always move.
A glove beneath the murk, palm-up,
waves goodbye, fingers clawing history.
Then another follows, middle finger
cursing the thousand cranes
stacking stone and steel.
A shuttlecock glides past, shot by the loser.
Cans, cups, a condom, a plank
float beneath this bridge of lost heads.
On the bank, old cobblestones
submit to further smoothing
and dead players stick forever

on lines they could not recall as
Sunday carries Saturday's trash and
drunken joy toward silence.

10. *Woman Puking in Front of Harrods*

It's ninety-two degrees in Londinium today,
a sweaty, sticky heat that crawls
out of the Thames, fanned by pigeon wings
into a viscous miasma.

I've walked the city, river to gritty
outlying boroughs, ridden sweltering trains
into Victorian-era depots, bricks grimed
with coal smoke and the last hope of

ancient prostitutes, broken purses
filled with gray sorrows. The echo of
Nazi bombs, absorbed by glass plinths,
still reverberates down old alleys.

On Brompton Road, the red palace
of perfume rises, concealing its orgy
of foreigners, plastic weapons trembling.
I wander in, just to say I did,

and regret it instantly; a hulking guard,
biceps big as melons, insists
he must search my pack, finds
maps, wrappers, this shabby notebook

(but he doesn't read the poems). Children
of privilege move among the glitz,
faux gold, mirrors and tile, aisles become
banks of a river where I flounder.

I escape through a beckoning door,
a portal back into the heat. Relief.
I've gone but a few steps when I see her,
a woman, stick thin, leaning over a

newspaper rack, puking into the street.
An older man hurries to help her—father?
He dabs drool from her lips, firm hand
on her bent brown back, face sad and

patient. It's what I want to do—
comfort her, make sure she doesn't
lurch forward into a taxi's path
or collapse onto filthy flagstones.

Go ahead, I murmur, as she heaves,
void all the excess of this place,
empty the expensive lunch right here,
or turn, if you can, and spew it across

glittering windows, splash it on the
shop cop's shined shoes, or stain
a mannequin's fancy dress and coat,
or dull the sheen of fine jewels.

I'm sorry for her suffering but not
for the truth she's revealed. This poem
is my souvenier, purchased with a pencil,
free for both of us after her refund.

11. Weaving Woman Haiku

The street is her loom.
She shuttles, pulling nightmares
behind, to bind day.

London, were the bombs'
concussions enough to wake
ancient kings in tombs?

Five millennia
these stones have stood on your hills.
Street person—don't care.

12. Poem for Goodbyes

I walked the streets and came apart,
pieces scattering like coins, glittering

on pavement, star's cold fire
sparking a loosed tongue to

learn another language, consonants
stacked in pairs and trios

spilling the stone circle's secrets,
scudding as a cloud does across

crumbled battlements, the soldier's
shivering misery, the pooled blood

on smoothed steps, steam
from the caldarium rising

to join sea fog and miasmas
off a foul trench. My eyes

freed from lid and nerve, saw
the past as though the sun

had never set, as though no new grave
were dug in rocky soil

of a dim churchyard. Was it death
rising from a vault to spear

the woman falling into
her lover's arms? He tried to shield her,

in vain. I removed my shoes
and stood barefoot on slabs

to hear the inscriptions faintly hum
to my bones from the bones below.

I read aloud the poems
left behind by poets

who knew best how to cling
to life, brief and green.

My ears, pressed to beech and oak,
heard songs sad enough to

slow the River Swale, vibrate
the barrow mound as ghosts

of kings and slaves let harmony
breathe again through their lips.

Tonight, before I leave, let me
walk with Blake down a street

narrow and dark, weeping for
a child long vanished, and he

will take my hand, call me friend,
and walk me homeward.

Thread of the Real

Poems by Joseph Hutchison
Colorado Poet Laureate

978-0-9713678-5-2

The thread of the real
strings our words like beads
together, loops them
around our lover's neck—
they kiss her when she walks.

Or say it's a line of mindfulness
that curves between differently
grained materials, a strand
of cloudy glue squeezed clear
between inlays of rosewood
and blond bay laurel. . . .

Umbrellas or Else

Poems by J. Diego Frey

978-1-938633-47-8

Chock full of laugh-out-loud poems, *Umbrellas or Else* blurs the line between the absurd and the profound. Poetry will never again be the same.

> *Tell of a self*
> *upended by rain.*
> *And the forest of kelp*
> *that grew up in my brain.*
> *In the night comes your yelp*
> *(as we circle the drain):*
> *"Umbrellas or else—*
> *we will sing it again!"*

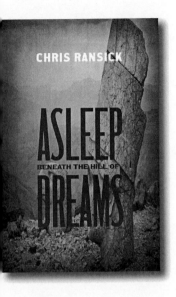

Asleep Beneath the Hill of Dreams

Poetry by Chris Ransick

978-1-938633-49-2
$12.99

Chris Ransick, appointed Denver Poet Laureate in 2006, is the author of five books: *Language for the Living and the Dead; Never Summer, Poems from Thin Air* (Winner of the Colorado Book Award); *A Return to Emptiness* (Colorado Book Award finalist); *Lost Songs & Last Chances*; and *Asleep Beneath the Hill of Dreams*.

MORE GREAT BOOKS FROM CONUNDRUM PRESS

Language for the Living and the Dead

Poetry by Chris Ransick

978-1-938633-15-7
$14.99

Chris Ransick has "something to say"–something important–about life's cruxes, what he calls "the wounding moment." Despite his intimations of mortality, it is the comfort that ilngers: "I would pick apples with you on our last day / and be filled up and satisfied."

—David Yezzi, author of *Birds of the Air*